DATE DUE			

THE SEASONS

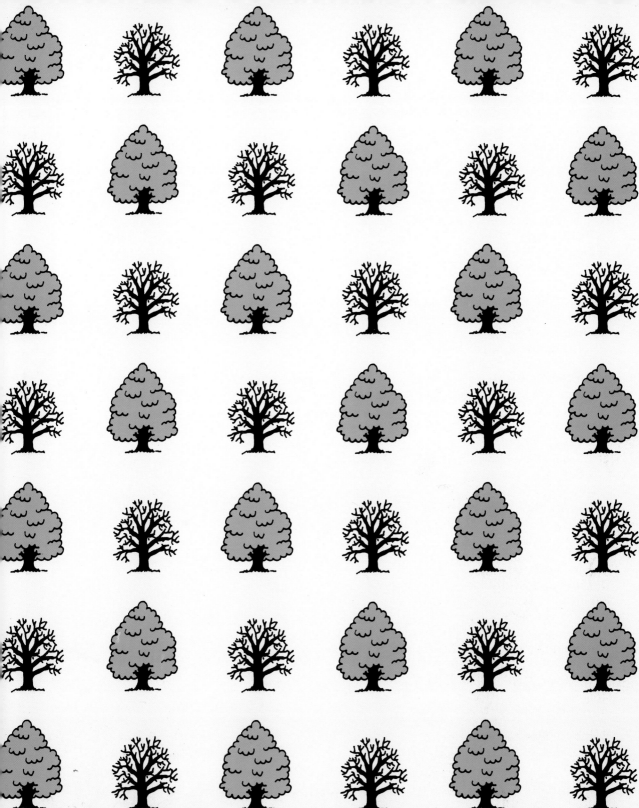

First published in the United States
in 1992 by Franklin Watts, Inc.
387 Park Avenue South
New York, NY 10016

Library of Congress Cataloging-in-Publication Data

Richardson, Joy.
      The seasons/Joy Richardson.
          p.   cm. — (Picture science)
      Includes index.
      Summary: Describes the different seasons
   and how they correspond to the earth's relative
   position to the sun.
      ISBN 0-531-14158-6
      1. Seasons—Juvenile literature. [1. Seasons.] I. Title.
   II. Series.
   QB637.4.R53   1992
   525'.5—dc20   91-29100
                                                  CIP AC

Editor: Sarah Ridley
Designer: Janet Watson
Illustrator: Linda Costello

Photographs: Bryan and Cherry **Alexander 24;** Chris
Fairclough Colour Library 10, 13, 16; Robert Harding
Picture Library 9, 15, 21 (right); David Hosking 27;
ZEFA cover, 7 (all), 19, 21 (left), 23.

Printed in Singapore.

THE SEASONS

Joy Richardson

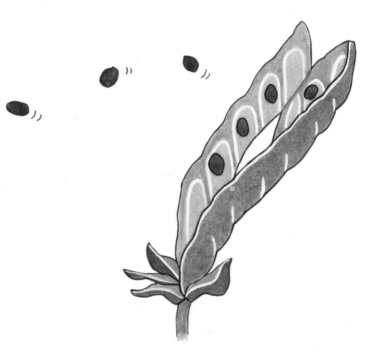

FRANKLIN WATTS
New York • London • Toronto • Sydney

A circle of seasons

Each year, we journey through the seasons as the earth travels around the sun.

Winter changes into spring,
spring grows into summer,
summer turns into autumn,
and autumn leads to winter again.

The seasons follow each other around in a circle.

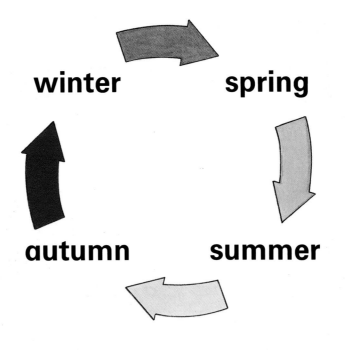

winter

spring

autumn

summer

Winter

In winter the air grows cold
and chills the earth.
Very little grows.

Frost sparkles on branches
and freezes the ground.
Snow tumbles from the sky.

There is less daylight in winter.

Squirrels and woodchucks go to sleep.
People wrap up warm to go outside.
Seeds lie waiting in the ground.

Winter is a resting time.

Spring

In spring the earth slowly warms up.
Warmth makes the grass grow.
Seeds crack open, pushing out new shoots.
Fresh green leaves uncurl from
dull brown buds.

Flowers bloom and bees buzz around them.
Caterpillars crawl from their eggs.

The earth is waking up again.

Summer

The weather becomes hotter.
The daylight lasts longer
and there is more sunshine.

The grass grows tall.
The trees are thick with leaves.

Wheat and barley ripen in the fields,
changing from green to gold.

Apples and plums grow fat and juicy
where blossom grew in springtime.

People like to be outside.
The summer is a good time for vacations.

Autumn

The green leaves change color
to yellow, red, and brown.

The leaves fall off the trees
and blow around on the ground.

Seeds scatter far and wide.

Empty fields are plowed up and
left ready for the next crop.

The ground is cooling off and
getting ready for winter.

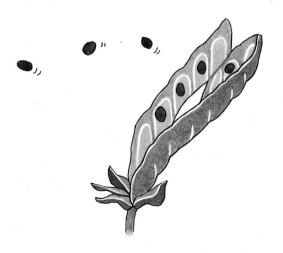

The sun in the sky

Each day, the sun seems to travel
across the sky from east to west.
This is because the earth spins around
once every day.

In summer the sun climbs high in the sky.
At midday it is nearly overhead.

In winter the sun stays lower down
as it crosses the sky.

This is because our part of the earth
points towards the sun in summer
and away from the sun in winter.

summer sun

winter sun

Journey around the sun

The earth spins around once each day.
It also travels around the sun each year
in a great big circle.

The earth stays tilted the same way
all the way around the sun.

While the north tilts towards the sun,
the south tilts away.
On the other side of the sun
it is the opposite way around.

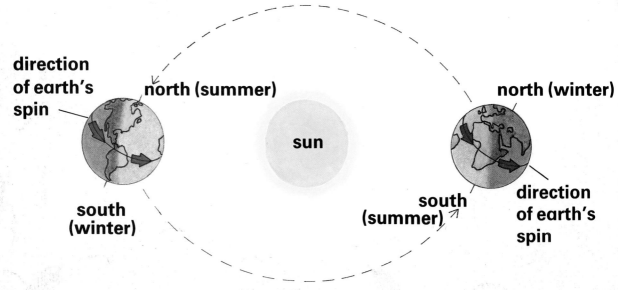

direction of earth's spin

north (summer)

north (winter)

sun

south (winter)

south (summer)

direction of earth's spin

north

south

Upside-down seasons

The seasons change as we change
our distance from the sun.

In January it is winter
in northern parts of the world
like Europe and America.
They are tilted away from the sun.

It is summer in southern parts
of the world like Australia.
They are tilted towards the sun.

It is very hot in Australia at Christmastime.

No change

The equator is a line marked on maps
to show the middle of the earth.
It is the imaginary line
dividing north and south.

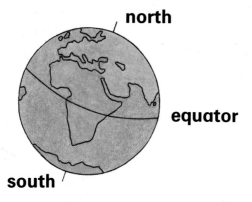

The equator is the closest part
of the world to the sun.
It stays the same distance
from the sun all year,
so there are no real seasons.

Most places near the equator
are hot all year around, and
the plants never stop growing.

Cold summers

The farther you travel from the equator, the colder the weather becomes.

In countries that are
a long way from the equator,
the winters are freezing cold.

The summers are warmer,
but not very hot.

In the far north and the far south,
the ice never disappears.

The pattern of the year

Some birds migrate with the seasons.
When winter comes,
they fly to a warmer country.

Most people stay in one place.
They change their clothes and
the heating in their homes
as the seasons come and go.

Wherever we live,
we get used to the seasons
that make up the pattern of our year.

January

December

February

November

March

What month
is it now?

October

April

Which season of
the year is it?

September

May

August

June

July

Index